# Leader's Guide

To Accompany

# THE CATHOLIC STUDY BIBLE

**Rev. Jim Nisbet**
*Old Mission*
*San Luis Obispo de Tolosa*

New York   Oxford
Oxford University Press
1990

Oxford University Press
Oxford   New York   Toronto
Delhi   Bombay   Calcutta   Madras   Karachi
Petaling Jaya   Singapore   Hong Kong   Tokyo
Nairobi   Dar es Salaam   Cape Town
Melbourne   Auckland
and associated companies in
Berlin   Ibadan

Copyright © 1990 by Oxford University Press, Inc.

Published by Oxford University Press, Inc.,
200 Madison Avenue, New York, New York 10016

Oxford is a registered trademark of Oxford University Press

All rights reserved. No part of this publication may be reproduced, stored
in a retrieval system, or transmitted, in any form or by any means, electronic,
mechanical, photocopying, recording, or otherwise, without the prior permission
of Oxford University Press.

ISBN 0-19-528393-7

Printing (last digit): 9 8 7 6 5 4 3 2 1

Printed in the United States of America on acid-free paper

# I

USING *THE CATHOLIC STUDY BIBLE* is an adventure in information. When I first saw the finished work, I could only think of the first time that I led a Bible Study. It was almost thirty years ago and it did not even occur to me that such a tool for study could ever be in my hands. The translation that I was using was terrible — the best available at the time, but terrible. Filled with thees and thous and using a style and vocabulary aimed at the people of England, it might as well have been written in a foreign language. There were some footnotes, as required in Catholic Bibles, but they were meant more to prevent some great misunderstanding than to help a student. There were two maps, simple line drawings, and no articles or introductions.

It was a time in our Church when people were just beginning to be interested in the study of the Bible and a small group formed where I was going to school. The leadership fell to me because I have always been passionately interested in the Bible, but I was no more qualified than any of the others. It was one of those situations where one knows too little to realize what is happening. The terror that began to overtake me about three days before the study only grew as I realized what I was about to do. As always, the Lord blessed the work in spite of me and we all learned. But as I look at the *Catholic Study Bible* I can only guess at the confidence such a tool could have given me.

The *Catholic Study Bible* is more valuable to the person who is better able to use it. So I would like to give a quick introduction to the use of this Bible. Everything that is mentioned in this section is available in other parts of this book as well as in the introductions in the *Catholic Study Bible* itself. However, here it is all presented in one short introduction.

# The Catholic Study Bible

## ARTICLES

The table of contents begins on page v. There is the first listing of articles: Introductory Articles and Reading Guides to the books of the Bible. On page viii is the second listing: Reference Articles. When preparing a study always quickly run through this list of topics. Often one or more of the articles will prove helpful in a specific study. Over a period of time, in using the articles, you will absorb the information and it will enrich all your Bible reading.

Each book of the Bible has two introductions. There is one at the beginning of the book itself and another in the Reading Guide section. When you are involved in the study of a particular book, it does not matter at what point you are in the book itself; it is very helpful to read both of those introductions. Like the articles, over time this information will be yours and easily available to you while you are reading the book. Often when I have found some difficulty in understanding a particular text and have not resolved my difficulty with the footnotes, I have found the necessary information in the introductions.

## TEXT

Now open to the first page of the Gospel of Mark (p. 68 of the New Testament). I will use this page as an example because most scholars believe that this Gospel was the first written and it begins right with the beginning of the ministry of Jesus.

The first thing to notice is the text itself. It is the Revised New American translation. It is written for people using American English and is very easy to read. For a person who is interested in the Bible this comes as no surprise, but for many people it is going to be a surprise. One of the facts of our legal system today is that Bible translations are copyrighted. When someone decides to publish a Bible, a choice of translations is made by the publisher. Often a publisher will choose an older translation because the copyright has run out and there is no charge to use the translation. This of course means that the publisher is then able to put more money into pictures, advertisement, or binding and keep the price of the book lower. The reason I am mentioning this is that often these

# Leader's Guide

Bibles are present in people's homes. They were purchased because they were inexpensive or beautiful but not because they were readable. If this is the sort of Bible that is in a person's home, any attempt to read the Bible is going to confirm that the Bible cannot be understood. When leading a Bible Study always point out the readability of the text itself; there are usually people present who have never experienced a modern translation. As I mentioned in the beginning, this text, even without any of the other helps in the book, would have made my first Bible sharing a much easier experience.

## READING GUIDE

Next I call your attention to the note in the left margin. The note is between two parallel lines right next to the first verse of Mark's Gospel. This alerts you to the fact that there is information in the Reading Guide that is going to help you. The appropriate pages in the Reading Guide are noted, in this case RG 408 - 410. The letters "RG" precede all page numbers in the Reading Guide. The Reading Guide in the *Catholic Study Bible* is in the section preceeding the Bible text itself.

## FOOTNOTES

Look at verse one of chapter one of Mark. There is an asterisk (*) after the number one and this indicates that there is information in the footnotes at the bottom of the page. The footnotes are clearly identified by chapter and verse numbers, in this case 1, 1 – 13. When reading the text watch for the presence of the asterisk and then read the corresponding footnote.

## GLOSSARY

Now look at verse two. In this verse is the word "prophet." When you come across a word in the text that is not usually used in daily conversation, this is a good time to check the Glossary, which begins on page 425 after the text of the Christian Scriptures. This word "prophet" appears on page 434. Even though you may know the meaning of the word, there is useful information in the Glossary that will enrich your understanding.

## MAPS

Notice verse five, which begins at the bottom of this first column. The verse mentions "the Judean countryside", "Jerusalem" and "the Jordan River." Any place name invites you to look to the maps in the final section of the *Catholic Study Bible*. There are fourteen maps covering the whole period of Bible History. The first map looks at the area in the thirteenth century B.C. The Jordan River was always there, but note that even the city of Jerusalem is present at this time. In fact, the city of Jerusalem appears on every one of the fourteen maps. On map number nine however, there are two views of the city itself, first in the period of the Hebrew Scriptures and second in the period of the Christian Scriptures. The maps even give a view of the city as it appears today in a light brown background. It is a useful map for someone trying to locate ancient sites in the city of Jerusalem today. These maps provide a view of the city in different periods of history and how the cities around Jerusalem came into being in one or another period and then were gone at other periods.

## GEOGRAPHY

But these geographical names also have another function. There is an article on the Geography of the Holy Land which begins on page 473. The reading of this article can help to give some idea of the weather and the plants and even some sense of how the place must have looked. The use of this particular article is going to greatly expand your ability to describe an event in an interesting way.

## CROSS-REFERENCES

Move on now to verse nine. After the verse number there is a small letter — here it is an "e." This indicates there is information in the cross-references at the bottom of the page. These are given after the footnotes and appear at the bottom of the page as a series of letters and numbers. These cross-references indicate other places in the Bible where there is similar information or a text that relates in some way to the verse being read. Here the reader is directed to passages in Matthew, Luke, and John, where each of these authors teach of the Baptism of Jesus. In this instance the reference is to parallel passages, but sometimes it is a prophecy or the fulfillment of a prophecy. Sometimes the references are to the Hebrew Scriptures and sometimes to the Christian Scripture and often to both.

The study of these cross-references can provide much information for some very interesting studies. The use of this information also helps people to understand the way in which the books of the Bible are related to each other, rather than thinking of them as isolated works. Personally, this was the feature of a Bible that I was the most reluctant to use because I was threatened by what appears to be only a list of numbers. However, with use this has become for me one of the richest tools in the Bible.

## HISTORY

Finally, I would point out one other thing, although as it happens there is no example of it on this particular page. Whenever you come across a name that is important in political history as well as Bible, it can be used to help date the material you are studying.

One of the articles in the *Catholic Study Bible* is "An Outline of Biblical History"; it begins on page RG 31. As an example I will take the name of Herod. On page RG 35 this article records that there are three people bearing the name of Herod and ruling during the life of Jesus. The Herod of the killing of the children of Bethlehem was not the Herod of the trial of Jesus. The names of political figures help date the material and also situate the story in events that were contemporary to the text.

I hope that this information is helpful as a beginning. Only over a period of time using this book will you come to realize just how much information is available within its covers and how easy it is to get at the information. I am sure you will discover many interesting ways to make your personal study more satisfying and, if you are leading a Bible Study, to make your presentations more interesting. The translation of the word Bible is library and with the *Catholic Study Bible* that is exactly what you have in your hand.

## II

**B**EGINNING A BIBLE STUDY has a lot in common with beginning a book. It seems to be rather simple until it is tried. The first study sets the tone for the whole series of studies. On the basis of the presentation of the first study people will either determine that they are interested and will make some kind of a committment to attend or decide that the study is not worth their time. Because of this the effort expended on the first study is more demanding than will be the rest of the studies and there are several things that are unique in the preparation of the first study.

### ADVERTISEMENT

The first study is the only one for which advertisement is important. After the first study people will learn of the sessions by word of mouth. People in attendance will enjoy or dislike the study and their commentary will bring people to the other studies. However, it is advertisement that is going to bring people to the first study. This is so important that for the first session I will usually plan the study in the light of possible advertising ideas. I pick a topic that may be particularly interesting to people in a particular area. The lesson on Jesus' first visit to Jerusalem which appears in the section on Lesson Plans is an example!

Advertisement is meant to draw people to the first study. The purpose of advertisement is not primarily information, but motivation. The information should be concise and clear. People need to know the time it begins and the time it ends, the place where it is happening and a title that is going to draw them to attend. For the advertisement to work it must be eye catching. Today we live in a

# Leader's Guide

world that has developed advertisement to a high art form and a little attention to the form that advertisement takes in our magazines and posters will provide interesting ideas. A typed page of information on a bulletin board is not really advertisement, it is more of a news announcement. Advertisement should be colorful and interesting; stark graphics really catch the eye. If you have any good ideas for some catchy advertisement, the first study is the time to use them.

## TEXT

Another peculiarity for the first study is that there can be no real preparation on the part of the people who come to the study. There is no opportunity to make some kind of an assignment for the people who will come. Yet it is a fact that when planning a Bible study a person must be aware that there are many people in our communities who have a long and varied background in Bible study, either alone or in other groups.

At the first session make it a point to tell people the particular translation of the Scriptures that you are using, the *Catholic Study Bible*, so that people who are interested in using the same text can acquire it. Mention this on the advertisement so that people can come prepared. Personally I enjoy comparing the different translations, to increase the richness of a particular text, but my experience is that people want to have the particular text that the leader of the study is using. Most bookstores will let you take some copies on consignment to sell to people at the first study. But it it also a good idea to have some copies that people may use at the study. This is a good practice to maintain throughout the study so that visitors can use these. This often makes them feel more comfortable and encourages their return as well as introducing them to the text you are using.

## SETTING

The setting for the Bible Study is a consideration for the first session and often it is a point over which there is not much control. Sometimes one is lucky to simply find a place to meet, such are the demands on meeting space at any parish where I have worked.

## The Catholic Study Bible

However, in the hope that there are some people somewhere who do have some choices to make in this area here are some suggestions.

A room that is too small is very uncomfortable and any discomfort in a setting translates into a difficulty in concentration. There are also people who will choose not to be involved in the study if it is uncomfortable and certainly as the study goes on, people who have one or another difficulty attending the sessions can find that the comfort of the setting may become the deciding factor in attendance. The room that is too small becomes doubly a problem when the weather is warm. It may be that in the end the number of people participating in the study will need to be limited in order to accommodate the room size. One of the more interesting things to notice in the teaching of Jesus is his movement from scripture interpretation, which took place inside the Synagogue, to parable teaching, which took place outside. It is not now possible to discover whether his moving outside drew the huge crowds that marked that period of his ministry or he moved outside to accommodate the crowds.

A room that is too large is not much better, but at least it is usable. There are few places in the world more depressing than an empty theater or assembly hall. The same impression is created by a small group of twenty people in the corner of a hall that seats six hundred people. If the room is too large, no matter how many people show up, it always looks as if almost no one is there. However, there are several ways to isolate a section of the room and create a smaller part of a large room, a more comfortable space.

Another factor in the choice of a room and the size of the room is the fact that there is really very little indication beforehand of the number of people who will attend a first study session. And in the chapter on "Continuing The Bible study," I will discuss the attendance cycle, which means that there is an anticipated change in the number of people attending a Bible study over a period of time. As much as possible the leader can try to make the study space comfortable to the number of people present. This becomes an easier factor to deal with after the first session. Perhaps the single rule for the first session is that it is better to have a space that is too large than to have a space that is too small. And in every parish there is usually someone who can give some kind of a guess on the number of people to come out for the educational events advertised by the parish. But remember it is at best a good guess!

Over the years I have also learned that there can be a number of unforeseen difficulties in particular spaces that were assigned to me for a Bible Study, difficulties that did not surface until I was in the space and the study was in progress. A room that is used by people who smoke, even though there may be no smoking at the study, can be very uncomfortable for people who do not smoke. And some of the most terrible looking rooms in the whole country are in parish plants. We give great attention to the Sanctuary and do a fairly good job there, but after that it is all downhill. Perhaps one of the greatest improvements in recent years has been the addition of beautiful study rooms in parish resource centers. These are places designed specifically for small group meetings and comfortable discussions. In time I am sure every parish will have such rooms, but for now I can only wish you luck.

## CHAIR ARRANGEMENT

Chair arrangement is another point that can appear to be rather straightforward and simple, but it is extremely important in setting the tone and nature of the Bible Study. The arrangement of the chairs in what I would call the classroom setting, with the chairs in rows all facing in one direction, is an arrangement that speaks of control. That is not necessarily bad. If the study is to be primarily a presentation then this is the best setting. It focuses everyone on a single point and concentrates the attention on the presenter. It creates a real distinction between the presenter, the one who is at the focus point, and the rest of the people. In any interaction that takes place in the group, the presenter is automatically involved. Questions and answers and even sharing among members of the group pass through the presenter in such a setting. Of all arrangements this is the one that makes it easiest to control a group and this is the reason that it is often used when teaching children.

The chairs may be arranged in a circle, what I would call the sharing setting. This arrangement speaks of equality. The leader is one among many and it is easy for the people to share directly with one another across the circle. It is a setting in which it is not easy to control a group and sometimes it can even be difficult to get the attenton of people in such an arrangement. However, this is the arrangement that makes sharing the easiest and it encourages participation on the part of the people. But one factor that may dictate the use of another form is the size of the group. When the circle becomes too large, the advantage of being able to share across the circle is lost and when there are several rows, one behind the others, the advantage is also lost.

A union of the two forms is the half-circle. In this setting there is enough of a chance to see most of the others in the group to encourage the sharing and yet the leader is clearly designated by the place facing the half-circle. This also retains an advantage of the classroom setting in that it allows the use of visuals, maps and a board, things that are difficult in the full circle.

Each chair arrangement has things to recommend it and some weaknesses. In my experience it is best to vary the arrangement according to the presentation each time. If there is a video, or map, then use the classroom setting; when the session is primarily sharing then use the circle. I am not trying to promote one form over another, but to explain that the setting of the chairs at the first Bible study is going to set a tone for the study immediately, before anything starts. Knowing this, the leader of the study is going to make some clear choices about sharing and control that are going to be evident to people at the first study even before the first word is spoken. People entering the room for the first time will know what they are in for and the leader needs to understand that the people are going to feel this.

## PURPOSE

The final point before the first Bible Study is the reason for the study itself. It is the purpose of the Bible Study that is going to determine the direction of the course and the subject matter to be covered as well as the focus of this first session. My personal goal in any Bible Study is to arouse an interest in the Scripture texts. I

## Leader's Guide

want participants to be able to read the Bible with confidence and be able to find helpful resources if they want them.

However, there can be many purposes for Bible study. In one small parish where I worked for awhile, it was the custom of the pastor to engage the congregation in a dialogue during the homily on Sunday. They wanted a study aimed at the texts for the upcoming Sunday or Feast, so participants would be more comfortable in the discussion. The advantage of the study was that there was never doubt about what was to be covered, but the disadvantage was that we were tied to four short passages from various parts of the Bible.

The purpose of a Bible study could be apologetic. Often members of a particular congregation are being challenged by members of another denomination and want to have a better understanding of their own tradition. But they want the understanding to be Bible-based so that the information can be shared with others. The truths of one denomination do not mean much to another Christian group when they are in the words of a theologian but among Christians the Scriptures usually carry weight.

Whatever the purpose, even if it is simply to provide Bible study, it needs to be stated and kept clearly in mind when planning the first Bible study session.

## III

**C**ONTINUING THE BIBLE STUDY becomes the focus of the leader's work, once the Bible Study has begun. In my experience the most important factor in sustaining any kind of a meeting is consistency. This is the maintenance of a large collection of seemingly unimportant details. These may seem to be very small things, but they prove over a period of time to be very important to the people participating in the study.

Consistency of time and place is the most important. For any person who has made the effort to free some time, get ready and go to the study only to find that the time has been changed, or the study has been moved or cancelled, the result can easily be an end of interest. There are many sacrifices that any one of us must make to be at any place regularly. Every second is accounted for in the life of almost everyone. To discover that the preparation was all for no purpose and the time has been wasted is often the deciding factor in any future attempt at attendance.

### PLACE

It is not possible to adequately prepare the people for any change. Often there are people who miss some sessions because of other things going on in their lives and they are not there at the meeting when the change is announced. For the life of me I do not know why the information printed in the Sunday bulletin reaches so few people, since they seem to read it cover to cover during my sermon. But you can be sure that no matter how well you have tried to make the change of place or time known, there is going to be some person who was not reached. Sometimes it is a person who has been planning for a long time to attend and has finally gotten everything together only to arrive at the empty room and probably never return.

When for some reason I have to be gone, I always try to schedule another presenter to lead the study in my place. This helps build involvement and prepares new leadership. It also ensures that there is someone there each week to greet the people. When there is a change of rooms, I always place a sign on the room that we have moved from for the benefit of anyone who arrives that night at the wrong room. And if we have been moved permanently to a new room, for at least five meetings I will have a sign on the door of the room where we used to meet.

## TIME

The time frame is a difficult problem because there are two very different elements that need to be taken into account. First, there must be a very clear understanding of the exact time the study will begin and end for the benefit of the schedules of the people who will attend. The study must begin on time, at the same time each session. Second, people also need to know when it will end because of the hiring of babysitters or the scheduling of transportation to and from the study. Some people may base their decision about attendance on their ability to clearly block a set time frame.

The other side of this difficulty is that there are very few people who are able to structure a study in such a way that it will begin and end exactly on time. Even if a leader has some special gift to allow for such scheduling, there is the unpredictable factor of the number and length of questions. The leader who is locked into some time frame may be placed in the position of feeling compelled to go on speaking after everything has been said. There is nothing more boring than listening to someone who has nothing to say but is filling time. There can also be the situation where the leader of the study has been so involved in questions that it is no longer possible to reach the intended point of the study in the allotted time. What I have found helpful is to schedule the study for exactly one hour, followed by fellowship and some refreshments. If I finish early, then we begin the fellowship early. If I find that I need more time, I stop at the end of the hour and invite the people to get some coffee and those who have some more time to join me for the finish of the study. This allows people who need to leave to do so without embarrassment, and gives me some more time. This allows the exactness of time frame necessary for scheduling on the part of the participants and the flexibility necessary for the presenter.

## ATTENDANCE CYCLE

The reason for making such a point of the consistency is the presence of the attendance cycle. I present this because it has always happened to me. With the first session people show up for a variety of reasons. Some are students and interested in theology, some are there because they are seeking a sharing group, and many attend because they are expecting some kind of a devotional experience. As time goes on people are going to discover if there is enough study to interest them or enough sharing to satisify them and many people are going to drop out. As the study grows smaller each week there is the temptation to think that there is something wrong and something needs to be changed. Be aware of the danger of changing the study to appeal to some person who has stopped attending. The missing person will probably not return and the people who have continued because they do like what is going on are then in danger of leaving.

Any Bible study is going to appeal to a certain audience and it is not possible to completely prepare people for the exact nature of a particular study. Many of the people are going to stop coming as the study goes on. It has been my experience that most stop coming. But as this process goes on, all the people who have not found what they are seeking are going to stop coming and finally the study is made up only of people who enjoy what is going on there. No matter how small that final number may be, once the cycle is complete everything that other people hear about the study is going to come from these people. They speak well of what they enjoy and the numbers will then begin to grow. Remember that, once the study is started, almost the entire promotion takes place through word of mouth. Even if you do some more advertisement, people who see the advertisement are going to talk to someone already attending.

# Leader's Guide

But be forewarned, the cycle takes about eighteen months and I think that there are not many studies that weather the cycle — most people get discouraged. In Salinas, California where I led a Bible study for about seven years, I started with about thirty people. Over a period of a little more than one year the number had dropped to six and we continued to meet, the six of us, for about two months. Then slowly the study began to grow and by the time I left Salinas there were about three hundred and fifty people involved in the study.

Accepting that this cycle is taking place can prevent some fatal mistakes. Do not presume that the lowering of the number of people means that you need to change the way you are conducting the study. The people who remain are there because they find something in the way you are conducting the study. Try to develop your presenting skills on the advice and suggestions of the people who are attending. And always remember that no matter the form of your presentation and no matter how good you may be at it, there are many people for whom it simply is not what they are seeking.

## STUDY FREQUENCY

The frequence of the study is also a point of consideration. The best way to maintain consistency is for the study to meet weekly. This is the form of planning that ties best into the scheduling of most people today. If the study meets at the same time on the same day of each week, there is the best chance for people to remember and the least chance that someone is going to show up where there is no study.

There is one weakness to the weekly study, however, and that is that many people do not want to commit themselves to anything every Monday evening for the rest of their lives. There are also some people who do not want to join in something that has already started. One way to handle this is to have the study weekly, but plan the study in blocks of six or ten weeks. Cover a set topic in six weeks and advertise the study in that way. Then people are able to commit themselves to the study and not think that it is a forever decision. This also provides for people who did not begin with the study, and do not like to join a study in progress, with a chance to enter at a new beginning. Another benefit of this approach is that there are now several first studies and there is the opportunity to advertise more often.

When a person does enter the study while it is going on there is a particular advantage to the *Catholic Study Bible.* The Reading Guide section is a quick and easy way to bring someone up to date on the story line. In many of the books of the Bible, like the books of Kings or the Gospels, the sequence of the story is very important. In this way the Study Guide can be used to make the newcomer more comfortable and more able to join in quickly. The leader has only to show the newcomer the text that needs to be read to catch up on the story.

The down side of weekly scheduling is that it is very hard on the presenter, particularly if there is a single person. The way I deal with this is to have some other people take some of the blocks and have others share in my block. That gives the presenter a few weeks off each year.

## GOOD NEWS

The Bible Study has a better chance of sustaining itself if the presenter is aware of the distinction between "good news" and "bad news." The "good news" is that the Lord loves me enough to save me. Any valid presentation of the teachings of the Bible is going to be a constant call to personal reform and the change in the way we live. This is certainly true in the teachings of Jesus. But it is also true that He always presented the truth in such a way as to make it "good news" to his hearers. In the case of the woman taken in adultery, Jesus did tell her that she had to change the way she was living, but not until he had guaranteed that she would not be stoned by the mob (John, chapter 8, p.161 of the New Testament). Jesus demanded everything of the Apostles, but first he asked them to travel around the country with him. In each instance Jesus invites and wins a person by the announcement of the "good news" for that particular person, and then he begins to demand the change. It is possible for the leader of a Bible study to begin by demanding change and in fact present "bad news." If one hears the "good news" first, then the person is going to change, but if the person hears the "bad news" first, that person does not wait around for the "good news."

The Scriptures show that the "good news" is always in terms that are important to the hearer. People need to know that the Lord loves and cares for them, that their salvation is the Lord's intention, that he is willing to provide everything to ensure that salvation, everything from forgiveness to strength. Only after that truth is grasped are people ready to accept that there needs to be change in their lives and then they are able to begin the process of personal reform. It is a very difficult line for the presenter to walk, but if one must err, best to err on the side of gentleness.

## INTEREST

In terms of sustaining the Bible study, the single most terrible crime of the presenter is to be uninteresting. I think that the great gift that the people in any Bible study give to the leader is that they do not have to be there and they have chosen to give the presenter this part of their precious time. And because their presence is always a personal choice made over many competing events, at each study they must be won again to make that committment for the following session.

The alert leader of the study constantly watches the group to see that the interest is sustained. When leading a Bible study I try to have a few things at hand to change the pace of the study if it appears that I am losing people's attention. Because my regular form of presentation is lecture, I keep some questions to use to spark some discussion because the joining of a discussion interests people. I try to bring some things that can be shown to the people or discussed. There is often an opportunity to have them refer to a map in their Bible. The maps are the last section of the *Catholic Study Bible*. To have some things like this on hand is to be able to change when interest seems to be dwindling.

## HUMOR

Another way to keep people interested is humor. In education I believe that humor is the honey that helps the medicine go down.

It is remarkable how often people who speak of a favorite teacher will mention humor. And humor is really very simple: it involves the presentation of a perceived incongruity. If people do not see the incongruity it is not funny. That is why there are so many inside jokes for doctors, mechanics or almost any profession. The listener must also know that the incongruity is obvious to the speaker. The telling of a joke is simply the setting up of a situation for the incongruity, then the presentation of the incongruity, the punch line. Often jokes are a distraction in a study. However, in the study of the Bible there is a built in incongruity because the world in which the texts were written is so different from the world in which we study the text.

When one uses humor in the Bible study, it will be more enjoyable for the students and spark their attention as well. Knowing that the leader is using this technique, people listen more closely so as not to be left out of the joke. When you describe Jesus doing his carpentry, add some electrical tools. When Joseph is seeking a place in Bethlehem, add some details peculiar to today's motels. In Bible study the possibilities are endless.

## BREVITY

Brevity is also important in teaching. In conversation most of us are fairly good at saying what we mean and getting an idea across in as few words as necessary. Yet when we write or speak before a group we seem to multiply words. The reason in my case is that I am seeking the best word or phrase to say something and seem to just keep adding words, using all the possibilities. Remembering our worst experiences with a teacher or a preacher most of us speak of people who simply could not stop talking. They were people who said the same thing over and over again in a hundred different ways until no one cared what they were saying at all. It is almost always best to say anything in the shortest way possible.

## IV

**P**LANNING AN INTERESTING STUDY requires the knowledge of some tricks. It does not just happen. One of the most helpful practices is to keep a mental notebook of what does and does not work in teaching. I often remember classes that I really enjoyed in my education and try to figure out what made them enjoyable and whenever I listen to any speaker in any situation I try to sort out what I like and what I do not. This memory of things serves me well in my own planning of the individual Bible study sessions. The following few paragraphs are a result of that memory.

The planning of the session begins with two questions. What do I want the people to learn? and what do I want to happen? Whether or not either of these is ever achieved is not the point, but unless one begins here there is no unity to the study. Often the session moves in a direction never intended by the leader and there is nothing wrong with that if the people are interested. Often people hear something completely different than was intended by the leader, and that is not necessarily bad. Most of the time people come and hear what they want to hear and what they need to hear at a particular time in their lives. All of this is beyond the control of the leader. But the use of a form of planning gives the leader some direction, a sense of confidence and unity to the session.

### SUBJECT

The question: "What do I want the people to learn?" concerns the purpose of the individual session and is often overlooked. Because most people are not professionally trained in the presentation of a class, this may not even occur to the leader. I think that the best preachers I have heard in my life have been teachers by profession and the reason they are so good at speaking is that they have some purpose or goal in what they say. Often I have listened to speakers who move from one point to another and never seem to go anywhere. The impression created is that the speaker is trying to fill a set block of time. It is not that the person did not say anything, it is just that there was no unity to the presentation. Purpose gives unity.

The purpose may be very simple, but beware of the purpose that is so general that it does not provide any help. If the purpose is only to study the Bible, there is no purpose at all. In preparation, the purpose allows the leader to choose and discard material based on where the study is going. It also provides some specific direction in which to move in the answering of questions. The reason that people trained in the presentation of a class are so good at this is that they usually present material with a view to getting some specific information back on an exam.

Usually my underlying purpose is to arouse an interest in the text so that people will want to return to the Bible on their own. I want them to know how much there is to know about the Bible and have them look at the text in a way that they may never have considered before. Yet none of these would serve in an individual session. Some things that I have wanted people to understand from a session are: Jesus was a human being just like we are; Mary needed a powerful faith to make the decisions she makes in the texts; the attack on the life of Jesus became inevitable as the ministry went on; Mark, Matthew, Luke, and John do not hold a single view of Jesus. There are many possibilities, but having a single purpose gives unity to the presentation.

## EXPERIENCE

The next question is, "What do I want to happen?" Do I want to have the people involved with one another in some kind of a discussion? Do I want to present a lecture? Do I want to have the people present a lot of questions? Any one of these can take place at the study; it is the choice of the leader. At the Bible study I lead,

## Leader's Guide

I want the people to have some experience of the world in which the texts were written.

I think that experience is the most neglected aspect of Bible study and because of it the words that are read do not often carry the feeling impact that they should. We all know what cinnamon is and what lamb is and most of the words we encounter are easily defined. But for anyone who has had any experience in the mideast, these words carry a strong feeling as well. For example, there are many spices mentioned in the Bible because the mideast has always been a great center for the trade in spices: even things not grown there are traded there. But when a person goes to buy spice in a mideast market it is not like anything that can be experienced in the western world. The spice merchants have their own street and there are huge bins of cloves, cinnamon, saffron, myrrh, laurel, and everything else you can imagine, along with many things you have never seen. The pungent smell of the spices fills the air and is almost intoxicating. You are caught in a huge crowd that is pushing, shoving, sniffing, and tasting everything. The entire mob is engaged in a communal discussion of the price and quality of everything with everybody. People will demand you taste something they are about to buy and insist on your evaluation, then ask your advice on the price being asked. Should you be seeking meat for some meal, the butchers also have their own street. It is not like going to any market, pushing a small button and being given a plastic wrapped steak on a styrofoam tray. The street is lined with shops in front of which hang identifiable carcasses and the butcher simply cuts you a slab from the area of the body to which you point. It is just as crowded as the spice market, but here the stench is terrible, the air is filled with flies and the street is running with blood.

In the parish in which I serve, we often invite a potter to sit in the sanctuary and throw pots while the Jeremiah passage about the potter is read (Jeremiah, chapter 18, p. 972 of the Old Testament). Watching the potter, the people are able to learn more than they possibly could from any explanation on the part of a preacher. If you bring spices to the study, remember that the ancient world did not deal in ground spices. They would be ground at home to prevent people from diluting the spice with something else. Bring

23

cloves, bay leaves, cinnamon bark and ginger roots. There are stones that remain simply words to people who have never handled them, but in every community in which I have ever been there are some people with huge collections of stones they are delighted to share. Most of the woods of the Bible are not the same as those we use, yet in every community in which I have been there are carpenters with access to every possible exotic wood. This type of thing is very interesting to people and provides a welcome change of pace from reading or listening. For the leader who is interested in doing this sort of thing there are precious few passages that do not provide some opportunity for an experience. This is also an area where people can be drawn into the study and persuaded to share information and resources with the others.

The most effective way to learn anything is always by experience. But the sharing of things is not the only way to experience the Bible. When I think back on my grade school religion class there is a single moment that sticks in my mind. One day the priest came to the third grade and acted out the Last Supper. We arranged the desks, and he assigned roles to everyone from Apostles to servers. The embarrassed nun was drafted into the role of Jesus — much to the amusement of the whole class — and the priest directed. I doubt if it was very good theater, but I also doubt if anyone ever forgot it. It was excellent teaching. If at all possible each session should include some experience. It may be something the people do or a demonstration in which they are asked to participate, but the key word is experience. Notice that Jesus spends much more time living with the disciples than he does teaching them and then when he does teach, he tells parables about the experiences that they have had.

## OTHER METHODS

The second most effective way to learn is by observation. Here I do not mean listening to something but watching something happen. Movies and exhibits are all in this area. But remember when the exhibit is passed around and people can touch it, you have turned it into an experience and given it more power. Observation

# Leader's Guide

is an area where people learn through things that are dynamic, while the participation of the people is not dynamic.

The third most effective way to learn is through static visuals. Examples would be maps, charts, pictures, etc. These things do not move and do not really involve us, but they are more powerful than words and often are the determining factor in our understanding of words.

Finally, the least effective way of learning is by listening to words, particularly words that are unaccompanied by any of the above. Yet for some reason most people seem to think that teaching is talking.

Every Bible study session should include these three elements. Something to experience: to see and touch, to smell or taste, something that physically involves the people at the study. Then there should be some opportunity to share: a chance to be the center of attention and offer insights or information to the others. And there should be something new to know, some reason for being at the study. The leader is wise to have these things at hand with some freedom, perhaps a question that will allow people to share or something for them to see or pass around. In this way, if during the presentation the leader notices that the attention of the people seems to be wandering, there is something to turn to. Change of pace is one of the best elements to keep people from becoming bored.

## RESOURCES

Caution should be exercised with the use of commentaries in a Bible study and by the leader as well. The plus and minus side of a commentary is the same: it is the work of experts. The plus is that it gives an educated look at the Scriptures, bringing archeology, science and the study of languages to bear on the text. But the minus is we presume that what the expert says is what the text means, and while usually true, it is certainly not all that the text means. The use of commentaries by people who are not themselves experts often gives the impression that they are not educated enough for the Bible to speak to them. Remember that the Bible was not written for scholars but for the believer. The scholars have much to offer, but the book is not theirs. Before consulting any commentary, I will always try to figure out what the text is trying to say and what it might particularly be saying to me. Only then do I look at the commentary. Also, never confine yourself to a single commentary, but always consult at least two. This is a great advantage of the *Catholic Study Bible:* it is the work of many scholars. There the text, the work of a translator, the footnotes, the introductions, the study guide and the articles as well each make a scholarly contribution.

Maps are one of the resources that are not often used with the creativity that brings the text to life. The *Catholic Study Bible* has an excellent set of maps. There are many geographical references in the Bible and it is often possible to map out a trip or pick out the locality of a particular event. The *Catholic Study Bible* does this with the Exodus (Map 2) and with the journeys of Paul (Map 14). But the leader of a study can often do this with many passages. The map showing the distance between Bethany and Jerusalem quickly shows why the raising of Lazarus in Bethany had such an immediate effect on the leaders in Jerusalem (Map 13). The distance between Bethany and Jerusalem, the temple, is about four miles, a one hour walk. The reference to maps at a particular study is both interesting and involves the people much more than simply listening to the lecture. Maps can show when a trip is uphill, long and difficult, or downhill and relatively short. It is possible to notice that people walking in a particular direction at a certain time of day are walking into the setting sun, as in the case of the people walking to Emmaus (Luke 24, 13ff, p.144 of the New Testament & Map 13). It is even possible to discover the temperature at a particular area by reference to the elevation indicated on the map and easier with some added information on the weather in a particular area at a particular time ("Geography of the Holy Land," p.473). One of the most important things to remember about maps and Bible language is that when the text says "go up" the meaning is uphill and when the text says "go down" the meaning is downhill. The people of Bible times did not use maps themselves, but because we are used to referring to maps we often say up when we mean North.

I think that the best formula for the beginning of a Bible Study session is first of all to welcome the people in some way and pray a short prayer. Then involve the people with some examination of their experiences. This encourages the people to share, involves them in the study and sets the stage for the Scriptural material to follow. This also lets the material that follows have some reference to their own lives. If you were beginning a study of the geneology material in Matthew and Luke, you might ask: "If you were writing your geneology is there someone you would leave out, or someone you would make sure was included?" (Matthew, chapter 1, p. 7 and Luke, chapter 3, p. 105 of the New Testament). Then have them share their ideas and they are ready to move into the study of the ancestors that Matthew and Luke chose to include. This type of an involvement question is an excellent beginning.

## HOMEWORK

The other side of preparation is the preparing of the participants in the study. The first form that this should take is the assignment of the Scriptural text or texts to be used in the study. However, I always read the text as a part of the study and never presume that it has been read. This is an aid to anyone who shows up for the first time and allows those who have pre-read to be better prepared.

I also consider it important to assign some other reading for the people to help them in a method of Bible study so that their study of the Scriptures is not tied to a particular Bible study style. Whenever possible I also try to make this assignment in their Bible. Few people are aware of the resource that their Bible edition can be. There are introductions to each of the books, and to each of the sections, there are footnotes, cross references, maps and even articles. I remember reading a small book when in high school. I finished the first chapter and went on to the next only to find it also titled "Chapter One." I was amused at the misprint and continued reading, only to find the author announcing that she never read introductions and in case the reader was of the same habit she called the introduction "chapter one" and now this second chapter was in fact "chapter one". After that I began to give greater attention to introductions and prefaces.

The *Catholic Study Bible* is edited with the intention that it should serve as the primary resource for a student of the Bible. There are many references and articles, all the work of excellent scholars who

## The Catholic Study Bible

knew that they were writing for interested students without a great formal background in scripture studies. The leader of the study can look at the resources available in the book and call these to the attention of the students as the best way to prepare for each study session.

The leader does not need to think that it is necessary to give less material to the others than the leader is using. The leader can easily stay far ahead of most of the others simply by making an effort to fully understand the material that is there, not just to read it. There is nothing in the whole world that better teaches a person about anything than trying to explain it to someone else. If the leader studies the material in order to present it to others, the leader will already be ahead.

As the leader, if you feel that you want or need some more information to prepare yourself for the study, there is some provided in the *Catholic Study Bible* itself. Each study guide section ends with a short list of additional books on the topic that is covered. Sometimes the list is at the end of a book like Isaiah (RG 304). Sometimes it is at the end of a series of books, as in the Wisdom Literature (RG 286).These books are the first ones that I would turn to in gathering information.

# V

**L**ESSON PLANS are not easy to prepare at first. But as time goes on the work becomes easier. The time and effort put into the planning of a study always pays off, if only in the confidence that it gives the leader. Even if there is no need to refer to the plan during the study, the knowledge that it is there gives confidence. To help the person who is new to lesson planning, I have provided a few samples built on the information given in the preceeding chapter. Over a period of time people usually develop their own particular approach to the material and the form of the study becomes more personal. But it is best to start with some standard form.

1. JESUS' FIRST VISIT TO JERUSALEM

    **Advertisement**

    Join Jesus on His first visit to Jerusalem

    **Purpose**

    Demonstrate that a Bible study can be interesting and different

    **Preparation**

    Pre-read all the Bible texts, with their footnotes and the page references to the *Catholic Study Bible* that are listed below.

    **Presentation**

    - (Turn to map 11) Locate Nazareth. Jesus would walk from Nazareth down to the foot of the Sea of Galilee and cross the Jordan. This would be done to avoid passing through the territory of Samaria, which was dangerous to the Jews ("Samaritan" in Glossary, p. 680; notes on Samaritan Woman, p. RG 500)

- Jesus would proceed south and recross the Jordan River near Jericho. He would then take the dangerous road to Jerusalem, mentioned in the parable of the Good Samaritan (Lk. 10:30-36). This road passed through Bethany into Jerusalem.
- (Turn to map 9) Jesus would enter the city through the gate between the Temple and the Pool of Bethesda (Jn. 5:2-9) after passing the Garden of Gethsemane. There are many places in the city of Jerusalem that figure in the ministry of Jesus; he could have visited any or all of them. He certainly visited the Temple, entering through the Golden Gate and going as far as the court of the Israelites (C of I on the map). (There is some information on Jerusalem archeology on p. 709).
- Several things that would probably have been new to Jesus were: crowds of sick or suffering, as at the Pool of Bethesda; trappings of civil authority for the Romans and for Herod; formal public worship in the Temple (Lk, 2:41-51 & footnotes); the international character of business in a large city

**Procedure**

The more details that can be added to the description of the trip, the more interesting it will be. There is a lot of helpful information in the article on "Geography of the Holy Land" on p. 713. Better to give more detailed information about one thing than to include many things. Have the people open to the maps as you speak.

**Sharing Question**

What impressed you most about a trip that you made early in your life? What do you think would have impressed you most about the Jerusalem of Jesus' day?

**Experience**

This would be the first visit of Jesus to an international spice market. Bring some Bible spices to touch and smell (cloves, laurel or bay leaves, cinnamon, saffron)

**What I Want to Happen**

I want people to spend a study with maps rather than with the text.

## Leader's Guide

2. ANNUNCIATIONS TO ZECHARIAH & MARY

**Advertisement**

When the angel speaks, one believes and another does not.

**Purpose**

Often the comparing of parallel texts enriches the understanding of each of the texts. (This is a basic theme of Luke.)

**Preparation**

Read chapter one of Luke, the footnotes and the Reading Guide (RG 469-478) as well as the introduction to the Gospel of Luke.

**Presentation**

- Read aloud Luke 1:1-4. Discuss Luke as a historian and contrast his introduction with the first few verses of Mark, Matthew, and John.
- Read Lk 1:5-23. Discuss the scene (this can be made interesting by the adding details you may know from reading or from pictures of the temple - the more vivid it can be made the more real it will appear and the more interesting it will become.)
- Notice the contrast between the reaction of Elizabeth to the pregnancy and the reaction of Zechariah to the announcement. Consider the reception of older women's pregnancies in their world and in ours.
- Read Lk 1:26-38. Discuss the scene. Contrast the reactions of Zechariah and Mary (note the similarity of the answer of Mary to that of Zechariah and the fact that the reason we know one is an answer of faith and one is not is the reaction of the angel).
- This is one of the most beautiful scenes and one of the easiest to elaborate upon in the entire Bible. Speak of Mary's confusion: she is a virgin. Speak of her fear: she is asked to be an unwed mother. Notice how human and natural everthing is on the part of Mary: she is any woman in that situation.
- Read Lk 1:39-45. Discuss the scene. Two women of faith, both pregnant for the first time. Mary is there in response to the angel, who offered the pregnancy of Elizabeth as the proof of the angel's words. There is a lot to be added to this scene by a woman sharing what it is to go through a first pregnancy with another woman.

- Read Lk 1:46-56. Compare this with the song of Hannah (1 Sam 2:1-10). Did Mary know the song of Hannah? Did the author of the Gospel have a particular reason to tie the words of Mary so closely to those of Hannah?
- Read Lk 1:57-80 Note that Zechariah's song follows the birth, while Mary's precedes. Faith enables one to sing the song of joy before the event takes place.

**Sharing Question**

Did you ever get some news that was so good, you had trouble believing it? Did you verify it?

**Experience**

Burn some incense and tell how it is used in the temple.

**What I Want to Happen**

I want people to see Mary's situation in contemporary terms.

3. JOB

**Advertisement**

Why do terrible things happen to good people?

**Purpose**

True wisdom is found in considering a question, not necessarily in answering the question!

**Preparation**

First read RG 257-266 and the Introduction to the Book of Job. Then read the Bible texts given below and the footnotes to the text.

**Presentation**
- Read Job 1:1-2:8. Talk about the situation (the difficulty of dealing with terrible suffering); about the setting of the court of the Lord (a rather typical Desert Sultan with members of the court); the fact that this is all simply the setting to discuss the problem.
- Read Job 3:1-19. Talk about Job's reaction to his difficulty, his sense of hopelessness. Remind the people that at this point in history there is little belief in everlasting life so reward and punishment must take place here, not in heaven or hell.

## Leader's Guide

- Read Job 4:1-6; 5:17-27. Talk about the advice of Eliphaz (either Job is being punished rightly or he has nothing to fear).
- Read Job 8:20-22. (The idea of Bildad is the same.)
- Read Job 11:7-12. (Zophar adds that perhaps the Lord knows about some evil that Job does not know).
- Read Job 16:2-5. (Job's response: they have nothing to offer to him). This is a good time to talk about how difficult it is to speak to someone who is in terrible trouble, to find the right words to say and actually offer some help. Consider the situation from both sides.
- Read Job 38:4-11; 40:1-9; 42:1-6. The Lord questions Job, but the only purpose of the questioning is to reveal the majesty and wisdom of the Lord, which is beyond understanding. Job is satisfied with the revelation of the Lord, although the question remains unanswered.
- Read Job 42:7-17 Here the ending indicates that the Lord is pleased with Job, although all he did was complain. The Lord enjoyed the fact that Job was talking directly to Him trying to get a hearing. He was not pleased with those who advised Job and were talking about the Lord rather than directly to Him.

**Sharing Question**
Think of a time of terrible trouble in your own life. Did a friend offer some help? Was it advice?

**Experience**
Turn off the lights and invite people to imagine themselves before birth with all the good and bad possibilities of life before them.

**What I Want to Happen**
I want the people to become comfortable with discussing a question that has no answer and realize how contemporary the question of Job remains.

# VI

**P**LANNING A COURSE OF STUDY is an especially good way (or tool) to bring new people into the Bible study. Today in our congregations there are many good people whose only acquaintance with the Bible is the readings used in worship. Their only education in the meanings of the text is the weekly homily. Many think that Bible study is a scholarly discussion about the meanings of Greek and Hebrew words. But if they can be shown that the Bible offers something interesting, they will attend.

There are people in our communities have a special interest in the saints. A course that is titled "Favored Saints" or "Saints of the Bible" could draw these people. The course might teach John the Baptizer or Peter the Apostle; either could easily involve two or three classes. All the material dealing with the Apostles might be covered in five or six classes. If you want to pursue either of these subjects, I would suggest that you read the Gospel account of Matthew and note each place where your chosen subject appears (p. 2 ff & RG 388 ff). Then if there is a parallel text in another part of the Bible it will be noted by a small letter that refers you to the cross-references of the page. Another subject of special interest to Catholics is the Virgin Mary. Several classes could be prepared from the material in the Gospel of Luke alone, but using the method mentioned above there is other material as well (p 95 ff & RG 417 ff).

This same approach can also be taken to a few of the people in the Hebrew Scriptures, particularly people whose names are common in our communities. David is an excellent example and a reading of First Samuel gives the life of David before he became king (p. 284 ff & RG 148 ff). Second Samuel records his life after he became king (p. 318 ff & RG 157 ff). Again pay careful attention to the reading guide, the footnotes, and the cross-references.

Another way to organize the study is around a specific topic. The sermons of Jesus, particularly as they are presented in the Gospel of Matthew, could provide many weeks of study material. These sermons are discussed in the Introduction, pp. 3 - 5. The parables of Jesus are scattered throughout the Gospels but there is a particularly rich collection of them in chapter 13 of Matthew (p. 28 ff). There are also several predictions of the passion and resurrection of Jesus and it is interesting to examine how and why they are placed where they are placed. The footnotes on Matthew 16:21 (p. 36), the first of the passion predictions, will refer you to the other predictions and the small letter in the text will refer you to the parallel texts in other Gospel accounts.

A course could concentrate simply on parallels, indicated by the small letters in the text. Few ever look at the Bible in this way. Parallel texts may be taken from the same book, as in the sample lesson plan dealing with the annunciations in the Gospel of Luke. But you can also parallel the same event in two different Gospel accounts. The Baptism of Jesus by John appears in three Gospels (Mt 3, 13-17 p. 11; Mk 1, 9-11 p. 68; Lk 3, 21-22 p. 104). The death of Jesus appears in all four (Mt 27, 45-56 p. 63; Mk 15, 33-41 p. 93; Lk 23, 44-49 p. 143; Jn 19, 17-30 p. 179,180). It is even possible to parallel texts in the Christian Scriptures with those in the Hebrew Scriptures; this is what the Church often does in the readings chosen for the Sunday Liturgies. Many of the cures of Jesus are the same as one worked by one or another prophet in the Hebrew Scriptures. The Liturgical texts are usually a great source of this material and on pages 452 - 466 is a complete table of the Liturgical readings.

One of my personal favorites is interpretations. This involves looking at some text in the Christian Scriptures that uses a text from the Hebrew Scriptures. The Gospel of Matthew and the letters of Paul are particularly rich in this material although it is rather frequent in all of the Christian Scriptures. Once you have chosen a text from the Christian Scriptures look up the quoted text in the Hebrew Scriptures. Here the footnotes and those small letters referring to the text numbers at the bottom of the page are helpful. Then study the context and the theme of the presentation in each of the texts. Here the Study Guide is helpful. This provides insight into the use of the Hebrew Scriptures by the early Christians. There are many surprises awaiting the student who chooses this path.

If there are people in a particular community who are considering a trip to Israel, an interesting course of study might involve many texts dealing with a particular city, Jerusalem being the best example. Another place that is particularly important to Christians is the town of Bethlehem, and it too is mentioned in the Hebrew as well as the Christian Scriptures. Many of the modern cities of Israel bear the biblical names again and this approach to a study greatly enriches a trip for someone who has a knowledge of these localities and events. An excellent way to conduct a study on such a topic is to ask each participant in a study to find one text involving the chosen city for the next study and then share and study the texts together. The most valuable resource for this study is the map section of the *Catholic Study Bible*

Sometimes a catchy question that people have heard on the lips of people attacking the Catholic faith brings in people who have been frustrated by such an attack. A study might be advertised with the question: "Did Jesus have brothers and sisters?" The starting point for this study could be Mk 6:1 - 5 (p. 76). The footnotes, the Reading Guide and the cross-references mentioned would provide enough material for a study. Another question could be: "Why do we call God Father and not Yahweh?" This would be covered by noticing the many texts where Jesus either speaks to the Father or speaks about the Father and noticing the words that Jesus uses. There are so many examples of this in the Gospel of John, you could read almost anywhere. Special attention should also be given to the Lord's prayer in both Matthew (6:5 ff p. 15,16) and Luke (11:1 ff p. 120,121). Notice that in the introduction to the prayer in both Gospels Jesus tells the Apostles how to address God. If people understand that the study of the Bible is going to prepare them to defend their faith better, many people will come to the study who have never considered it before.

# Leader's Guide

## SEQUENCE

Often a Bible Study goes through a verse by verse examination of the text beginning with either Genesis or Matthew and working through to the Book of Revelation. There is an advantage in this in that this is the way that the footnotes in the *Catholic Study Bible* are arranged. Once something has been explained in Matthew for instance, when the same topic is covered in Luke the reader will be referred to the Matthew footnote. But there are some terrible pits along the way. If one starts in Genesis, all should go well until Leviticus. However, this collection of ritual laws tests the interest of all but a dedicated student of Jewish custom. And even if one survives this there is the Book of Numbers waiting just a little beyond and there is nothing less interesting than a census.

A better way to design the course is to take a particular book and go through it from beginning to end verse by verse. But choose the books in a sequence that can build interest. There are many advantages to this approach over the move from Genesis to Revelation. In the way the books of the Bible are arranged today, they are grouped according to central topic. There are sections of History, Wisdom, Prophecy and others. Once the study is in one of the sections it is easy to become tired of the particular type of literature. Switching books is a good way to avoid boredom. In fact, if I discover that the people are losing interest, I try to change the topic either immediately or for the next study.

When beginning a study, I would suggest that you try a short book. I usually recommend Ruth (p. 278 ff). It is very short, easily one lesson. It is a beautiful story, no murder, no wars. Ruth also has the advantage of being one of the ancestors of Jesus, providing a subject of interest to people curious about the Hebrew Scriptures as well as to people interested in the Christian Scriptures. It is an easy book: anyone can read it in less than an hour. Between the Reading Guide and the footnotes, the customs are explained and there is more than enough material for a study simply in the Reading Guide. This is another story where a map will serve very well.

In choosing a particular book for the study, it is wise to read particularly the introduction to the book before even suggesting it to the group. Each of the books is easily placed in a certain area of subject matter and the whole nature of the study is going to be affected by that subject. A place to get some idea of what I mean here would be the Reading Guide, pp. 36 - 41, which discusses the different kinds of literature in the Pentateuch and how they relate to one another. A decision to study Joshua means that a good deal of time will be spent in the study of maps. And since it is a history book, there is going to be time spent on dates and contemporary events, information that is available in the Reading Guide. If the choice is made to study one of the Epistles, then there is going to be some discussion of moral issues. And if the Epistle is one of the letters of Paul there is also going to be some theology; again this is information available in the Reading Guide.

This approach of moving from one book to another through the Bible provides a chance for the people to become acquainted with the variety of literature available in the Bible as well as the different ways in which the authors deal with the topics.

## INTEREST

Finally, if you are leading a Bible study, whenever you are reading be alert to topics that will be interesting and eye-catching. Usually what is of great interest to you is what you will present with the most interest. One of the most wonderful things in the world is to listen to some small child explain his collection. The interest that the child has infuses the facts with such power that even things you already know are interesting from the child. Think of things that might invite people to the study and particularly topics that might appeal to people who are not yet involved in the study. Keep notes on this as you read your Bible. Also be aware of the timeliness of particular subjects. A study of the resurrection stories around Easter time is an example. Also, keep in mind that in the Catholic community it is the custom to do something special for the season of Lent and in many places Advent as well. If an interesting Bible study is promoted at these times there is a chance that some will consider it as a way of making one of these seasons special. Creativity in the choice and timing of topics is the best way to bring new people into the Bible study.

# VII

**LEADING THE STUDY.** Remember that the people are there by choice. There is a good side and a bad side to the fact that the people do not have to be at the Bible study. On the good side, the people are there because they are interested and they want to be involved. Each person has chosen to be there over somewhere else and each wants to have the study go well. This is unlike students in a mandatory class who often undermine that class to confirm the fact that they don't want to be there. On the bad side, the leader must win the people each time so that they will return. The study must be interesting; people will not return again and again to be bored.

## A STUDENT

For me personally, one of the most freeing attitudes to bring to the leadership of a Bible study is that I am one of the students. Escape the title teacher and you escape many of the requirements that seem built into the term. I invite the people to study the Scriptures with me and try to the best of my ability to lead the study. But the student attitude allows me to deal with the questions that I am not able to answer comfortably because I consider myself to be a fellow student helping another find the answer. The burden to have the answer does not fall on me. I can listen to the difficulties that people have with the text and share my own feelings and attitudes with the others without any sense that I have to defend the text. Frequently I remind people that while I want to understand and share the Scriptures, I did not write them. I take no responsibility for the strictness of Paul or the difficulties of the Hebrew Law. It is my opinion that when Jesus requested that no person

## The Catholic Study Bible

should be called teacher his concern was the burden that rests on the person bearing this title (Mt 23, 8 p. 50).

In any study of a subject that deals extensively with the written word, like Scripture or Law, it is more important to be able to find information than it is to have the information. The leader of the study would be wise to take every opportunity to become aware of the resources available in a particular area. Frequent local libraries; many churches have their own library or book rooms. Become familiar with the books that are carried in the local book stores, not ignoring the secular stores. There are a multitude of resources available to almost anyone anywhere today and one of the primary roles of the study leader is to make these known to the other students. The leader who is able to prepare the students to be able to study on their own without the leader is the best possible leader.

## FAITH SHARING

Make it a part of each Bible study to share your own faith in some way. The construction of the Scripture stories can often give the impression that if you have not seen a burning bush, heard the voice of the Lord from the sky, or been visited by an angel, then the Lord is not involved with you. There is a certain drama involved in an experience of the presence of the Lord, and it may not be present in any of the details of the story. The authors of the Scripture texts are many times at pains to construct a story so that not only the event but also the emotional impact on the participant is carried in the text. The result of this is that people can think that they are much less involved with the Lord than they really are.

By sharing personal experience of the Lord in our own lives we are able to give a more modern and immediate account of the presence of the Lord. People in a Bible study usually are seeking a greater involvement with the Lord and many are there particularly because they want that involvement to be Scripturally based. There is a special power that is carried in the sharing of actual involvement with the Lord. The caution here is not to over-dramatize or elaborate to make it "sound better". Often when this is done people are aware that it is happening and reject the whole thing. It also enforces the idea that if there is not something very unusual then the Lord is not involved. I think that some of the strange stories that TV evangelists have sometimes told about their own experiences would have less negative influence on people if most understood how simply and easily the Lord usually directs people. Sharing your own faith life will also encourage others to share theirs.

Allowing the time for people to share and creating the situations in which they are encouraged to share is another whole area of Bible study. The larger the group, the more difficult this is going to be, although one way to deal with a large crowd is to break into smaller groups for sharing. Sharing is encouraged first of all by the attitude of the leader. A group early on clearly understands whether or not sharing is welcome by the encouragement and reception that it receives. If people feel that they will have to defend themselves, or that they are going to be judged in some way by their sharing, it will not happen. There is a certain type of question that greatly encourages sharing and it is the question that is personal to the lives of the students. As an example, if the topic is Passover, ask: "What is the day to which you look forward with the greatest anticipation each year?" There can be no wrong answer to the question and people feel free to share. Also with such a question the amount of sharing is open to the speaker. The answer can be as simple as "Christmas" and can include why it is special and the preparations necessary for the day. Such questions are the handiest tools for sharing.

## ON TRACK

One of the main concerns of any study leader is to keep people on the subject. It is a trained ear that knows how much personal sharing is going to lead into the subject and involve the students and how much is a wandering away from the point. There are all kinds of distractions that can intrude on the study, but the leader watches for them and brings the people back to the topic. The longer one does this the better one becomes at it. Again because this a voluntary group it is easier to accomplish than in the usual classroom setting. I do not know of a single adult who does not cherish the memories of leading teachers farther and farther away from the topic in school. But no matter how interested or dedicated the group, unless there is a leader guarding against the wandering, it is always a danger.

Continual reference to the particular text being discussed is one way of keeping people on the topic. The leader is cautioned here also that the return to the topic is best accomplished in such a way that it does not appear a correction of some person in the group. One of the easiest and most comfortable ways for me to return to the topic is to continue a discussion and then interrupt myself with the question: "How did we get here?" — and then return to the Bible text. This is another example of not becoming a teacher. Here we are all at fault, not a teacher correcting some students. The most important aspect of this is that I have interrupted me, not one of the other students.

## PRIDE & ENVY

Two great enemies of the leader of a Bible study walk hand in hand. They are pride and envy. Pride is a concentration on the self and how I appear in the group. It can make the whole of the study revolve around me rather than the text and can also make the sharing of any other person an attack. Pride prohibits me from learning from others and often from even listening to them. It is a very difficult thing to put my finger on, but it is very clear to the people studying with a person suffering under the burden of pride. I remember once when doing a presentation to a large group, someone asked a question and I answered it, concluding with the question: "Does that answer your question?" The response was "No!" The temptation was to simply smile as though the questioner was not capable of understanding and then move on to the next question. But the proper thing to do was to seek again to understand the question. I have found that everyone is more comfortable when I assume that I have misunderstood.

The other enemy of the Bible study is envy. I think that envy is the enemy of all learning. If my attitude in the study is colored by envy it is not going to be possible for me to allow anyone else to appear brilliant unless of course I can make it appear that they are just slightly less brilliant than me. Envy allows a leader to dismiss the contributions of others with: "I mentioned that earlier" or "I would have shared that if I had considered it important." It does not take much envy on the part of a leader to destroy the sharing of a group and prohibit the contributions that could enrich the study and the understanding of the leader. When I am leading a Bible study, I will ask a friend who is attending to watch for pride and envy and call me on it.

## CLEAR MEANING

Finally, concentrate on the clear teaching of the text. Often as a leader I would like to tell the people something totally new. Yet there is a clear teaching in each passage and that is what the study seeks. I remember a teacher talking about the miracle of Jesus walking on the water (Mk 6, 45 ff p. 78). I think that the idea in the mind of the teacher was that there was no miracle, although then it is difficult to imagine why the author would have wanted to include the story. The teacher told us that Jesus was able to see the Apostles being tossed around by the sea of Galilee because he was on a hill and the night was so clear. Then the Apostles thought that they saw Jesus walking on the water, although he was actually on the shore, because the fog was so thick that they did not see the land. It would have been good for the teacher to have heard what the people were saying about the study later.

Often there are some fascinating ideas and insights to be brought to the study and people come to the study to do more than have the text read to them. But the first order of the study is the clear meaning of the text and no matter what is added and shared, remember to begin and end with that meaning.

# VIII

**D**IFFICULTIES can be avoided with a little planning. There are several things tot be aware of in any Bible study today. The first is that there are always people of many different religious denominations present. In the explanation of a particular text be aware of the different backgrounds. The fact that the study takes place in a Catholic parish means that there is going to be a Catholic view. But no person should feel that their particular denomination is going to be attacked at the study. As Peter reminds us in his letter, each person should have reasons for the hope that is held (1 Pt 3,15 p. 379). Each person should try to understand how particular beliefs flow from the Scriptures. There is no real problem with different explanations of a particular text from different backgrounds as long as no person needs to refute or attack another view.

This ecumenical nature of Bible study is one of the gifts of the Second Vatican Council. There is a great desire in the Christian community not only to understand the Scriptures but also to understand the beliefs of other denominations. If we are able to share our beliefs in the light of the book we hold in common, we have worked for the reunion of all believers.

## QUESTIONS

Be aware that questions can be either a tool of study or a distraction. In my reading of the Scripture texts, I am amazed at how seldom Jesus will directly answer a question. More often than not he changes the question and then answers. I think that the reason for this is that there is more wisdom in a question than there is in an answer. Remember the incident when, in the presence of the man with the withered hand, Jesus was asked whether one was permitted to work on the Sabbath. Jesus changed the question to whether one did good or bad on the Sabbath (Mt 12, 9-14 p. 26 & Mk 3, 1-6 p. 71). If the question is whether one can work, there can be no cure. If the question is doing good or bad, then one has to cure. In this situation it was the question that really determined the action. A question sets the limits in which an answer can be given. A leader is wise to carefully listen to each question to discover whether it should be answered, analyzed, changed or simply passed over. I think that the power of the question is something that is very neglected today. The very first time that the great wisdom of Jesus was noticed was when he was asking questions of the Scribes at the age of twelve (Lk 2, 41-50 p. 103).

When a question is answered it must be without an attack. While the leader may wonder whether or not the question is intended as an attack, this can be ignored in the answering of the question. Often this has the effect of calming even the person who intended to attack. There is often the temptation to make a questioner look stupid or uninformed, but there is no benefit to this. Answer a question clearly and directly, avoiding any unnecessary attack.

## ARGUMENTS

It was mentioned above that the leader needs to watch for and prevent an argument. The internal flaw in the argument is that it requires two people and if one person refuses to participate then the argument is over. Remember that it is not necessary to win an argument, only to end it. There are two signs of a developing argument. The first is that there is no new information being added to the discussion. When one or both of the parties are simply repeating what has already been said, then the argument is starting. The other sign, and this is infallible, is that there is a steady rise in both the volume and emotional level of the participants. The longer one is leader of a Bible study the earlier in the process one will recognize the argument and the easier will be the escape. Remember always that there is no need to win the argument, but there is the responsibility of the leader to end it.

## CAREFUL WORDS

Be careful about contradicting the faith of the people attending the Bible Study. If you are considering the life of Peter as it is presented in the Bible, you quickly notice that there is no indication that Peter was crucified either upside down or rightside up. It is easy to say that Peter was not crucified, but that is not correct. The fact is that the Bible neither supports or denies the fact of the way Peter died. That information has come from tradition and not from the Bible; the Bible just says nothing on the topic.

Try to avoid words that do not teach. The whole purpose of teaching is to give new information in a way that is understandable. When I first began to study Scripture in the seminary it was a long time before I was able to catch on to the vocabulary. Today this is a particularly difficult problem in our world. Every profession seems to have a special vocabulary that makes it difficult for one who is not in the field to understand what is happening. Often I feel that it is a smoke screen for something that they do not want me to know. Both my doctor and my mechanic speak a language I never learned in school. It is easy to slip into a special language in Scripture and that is great, even necessary, if your intention is to become a great scholar. But that language is a hindrance if your goal is sharing with others. Always ask yourself, "Am I clear?" It helps to often ask the others in the study if what you're saying is clear.

The principal idea behind the *Catholic Study Bible* is to take the learning and understanding of great scholars and render it in the language of the student. The more one reads and uses the Reading Guide and other materials in the Bible the better one will become at this. There is a real art to being able to take deep and powerful ideas and present them in a clear and understandable way. This area of speaking in words that are clear is another place where I ask someone in the study to listen and report to me.

## TRUE TEXT

Be very careful of ever using one text against another. In Catholic tradition there is a very special place that is given to the Gospels. We use a more beautiful book, sing a verse before reading the text

# Leader's Guide

in the Liturgy and carry the book in procession. But we do not maintain that the Gospel is any more inspired than any other part of the Bible. It is all the word of the Lord.

There are several factors that influence the differences that appear in the text and often the study guide will sort these out. I remember a professor in Bible class describing the problems of a particular book by saying: "The author spoke Aramaic, thought in Hebrew, wrote in Greek, and you are studying it in English."

Besides the language problems there are time problems. Often the text is written in a world that is very different from that in which the event took place. Sometimes the story has passed orally through more than one culture before it is finally rendered in the written form. One example is the struggle of Jacob. In one place the struggle is with an angel and in another place it is with a man and in two others with God (Gn 32, 25; 32,31 p. 41 & Hos 12,4; 12,5 p. 1119) . The Bible question is not whether the struggle was in fact with an angel, a man or with God, but rather why did one author in one time and place write God and angel and the other write man and God.

## CATHOLIC STUDY BIBLE

During the Bible Study make frequent references to the *Catholic Study Bible*. It is in the Bible study that the people are going to learn how to use the resource. It is more important for people to learn to study the Bible than it is for them to learn the individual lesson. If they learn to study, then Bible study will continue for a lifetime. Constant reference to the *Catholic Study Bible* will acquaint them with the amount of material there.

Make the references to the text as varied as possible. It is easy enough to refer to the Reading Guides or the footnotes. But it is the use of the maps and the articles that will teach people how to use the resource. Try at each Bible study to make at least two references to information in the book that is neither in the footnotes nor Reading Guides. Referring to this material as a way of preparing for the next study will also encourage people to use it.

One of the most valuable articles is the "Outline of Bible History" (RG 31). No matter what Bible text you are studying the events took place at some time in the Bible's history and often its writing is situated at another time. A quick reference to this short article allows the student to place the event and the writing in the whole spectrum of Bible History. I think that this is particularly important for us today who do not study the events in sequence but skip around in our reading. Without this kind of reference it is easy to lose the relationships between the many different texts.

Read the introduction to the particular book to discover the date of the material covered and the proposed date of the composition of the work. In the "Outline of Bible History" you will find information about the periods indicated by the dates.

Watch carefully to discover if people are becoming bored with the topic. It may be that once you have gone through a few classes on some topic it is not as interesting as you thought or not as interesting to the others as to you. Do not be afraid to abandon some topic and start another. The interest of the group is of the greatest importance. The study of Scripture is not a matter of covering all the material; it is a matter of continuing the study. I think that the Lord is going to ask me if I am involved in the study of his word, but he is not going to ask me how far I got in the book.

In conclusion, are very few things in this world that are more rewarding than leading a Bible study. There is a great investment of time. There is the great vulnerability of being in front of a group. There is the difficulty of trying to understand the texts that have baffled and delighted the greatest minds of history. But there is the reward of being about something that is of the greatest importance. When I attend a Liturgy and watch the vested Deacon incense the Gospel Book as the choir sings, I am reminded of the importance of this work. When I visit an art museum and look at the bejeweled, enameled covers created for the Bibles of old, I am reminded of the importance of this work. When I read of the lives of the martyrs, who considered it an honor to die for the truths contained within the Bible, I am reminded of the importance of this work. And when I remember the final command of Jesus to his small band of faithful followers, "Go out and teach....," I am reminded of the importance of this work.